MAELLE

THE PEOPLE'S

PRINCESS

The Story of a young African princess defying the odds during slavery time, to become an unexpected heroine

Written by Emmanuel Bichotte

Co-Written by Maelle, Elijah Bichotte

PREFACE

I want to thank my Lord and Savior, Jesus Christ, for the gift of creativity. I want to thank my wife for her love and support, my older daughter, Megan (23), brothers Rodriguez (21), and Elijah (12). I specifically want to thank my youngest daughter, Maelle (10), without whom this story would never see the light of day.

Maelle once asked me, "Daddy, how come Disney does not have many black princesses' movies?" I answered, "It'sprobably because there aren't too many interesting stories about black princesses." So, she thought and said,"Well, when I grow up, I will write the most interesting story about a black princess."

I told her she doesn't need to wait until her adult age to write the story. I encouraged her to write one now. Two weeks later, this story began to take shape. She came to me and declared, "Dad, I have an idea. I will write about a princess who fought against slavery in Africa, with her thoughts and not guns." I was taken aback and questioned her idea.

She went on to say, "Yeah, dad. I will write about an African princess who outsmarts the slave traders just the Harriett Tubman lady outsmarted the slave masters to free many slaves without shooting anyone." Her idea impressed me that I promised to help her write the story. Eventually, I ended up writing the whole story. However, her ideas alone made this book a possibility. Thus, I am thanking Maelle and Elijah for being my sounding board and source of inspiration for this book.

Lastly, certainly not least, I would like to thank my brothers and sister, who have been the rock on which I stand. My late brother Johnny K Bichotte, Patrick Louis Jean, Menahem B. Bichotte, Yohanan Bichotte, Ben Amy Bichotte, and Myrline Jean Louis. I say thanks to you all.

HISTORICAL BACKGROUND

The idea for this story originated from research regarding slavery in Africa. This took place in West Africa in the 18th Century. It was when free African men were taken from West Africa to become slaves that are sold into slavery to European traders for the Americas and the Caribbean.

Referred in Wikipedia as *"The Middle Passage, which was the crossing of the Atlantic to the Americas, endured by slaves laid out in rows in the holds of ships, was only one element of the well-known triangular trade engaged in by Portuguese, Dutch, Danish-Norwegians,[41] French, British and others. Ships having landed slaves in Caribbean ports would take on sugar, indigo, raw cotton, and later coffee, and make for Liverpool, Nantes, Lisbon or Amsterdam. Ships leaving European ports for West Africa would carry printed cotton textiles, some originally from India, copper utensils and bangles, pewter plates and pots, iron bars more valued than gold, hats, trinkets, gunpowder and firearms and alcohol. Tropical shipworms were eliminated in the cold Atlantic waters, and at each unloading, a profit was made.*

*The Atlantic slave trade peaked in the late 18th century when the **largest number of slaves were captured on raiding expeditions into the interior of West Africa.** These expeditions were typically carried out by African states, such as the Oyo empire (Yoruba), Kong Empire, Kingdom of Benin, Imamate of Futa Jallon, Imamate of Futa Toro, Kingdom of Kaya, Kingdom of Kasson, Kingdom of Kaabu, Fante Confederacy, Ashanti Confederacy,*

Aro Confederacy and the kingdom of Dahomey.[42] Europeans rarely entered the interior of Africa, due to fear of disease and moreover fierce African resistance. The slaves were brought to coastal outposts, where they were traded for goods. The people captured on these expeditions were shipped by European traders to the colonies of the New World. As a result of the War of the Spanish Succession, the United Kingdom obtained the monopoly (asiento de negros) of transporting captive Africans to Spanish America. It is estimated that over the centuries, twelve to twenty million people were shipped as slaves from Africa by European traders, of whom some 15 percent died during the terrible voyage, many during the arduous journey through the Middle Passage. The vast majority were shipped to the Americas, but some also went to Europe and Southern Africa."

CHAPTER 1

The Kingdom of Libertia

It all began in a kingdom in the heart of Africa.In a place called Libertia, reside in a beautiful royal palacea one of a kindroyal family: King Jahjah, Queen Meme, and their beautiful daughter, princess Maelle. King Jahjah and Queen Meme were very much adored by the subjects of the kingdom of Liberia but not so much the princess.

The kingdom was a beautiful place in the middle of the forest, with beautiful rivers ending in the most breath-taking water cascade. Everyone lived in peace and harmony with each other and with the neighboringkingdoms. Indeed, the people loved the king and queen, but they did not hate the Princess theysimply were not too fond of her ways. Some of her subjects believed she was just an evil brat, and others believed that she was just evil. Their sentimentswere that she only cared about herself and no one else. She was not fun to be around, and she liked to make fun of people, she liked to put them down. Yet she did not like seeing her people suffering at the hand of others. She may not have seemedto be too friendly to them, but she detested witnessing her people suffering at the hand of any others.

Her relationship with her people certainly a complicated one. The truth is the princesswasn't aware of how her subjects felt about her shedid not care much about how they felt about her.

Unfortunately, even people from the outside noticed that strain between the Princess and her people. To most Princess Maelle was known to be the meanest of the royal family.

One night while she was sleeping in her richly and beautifully decorated room, she had a dream.She saw herself standing in front of her subjects, and they were applauding her and waving at her lovingly.She was happily waving to back at them. All of a sudden, the people's faces in the crowd started changing from smiling to severe, then to being mad.Then, a voice called out from the crowd and said, **"LET'S GET HER!"** They started coming towards her, her guards stood their ground to protect her, but the crowd was too many for the crowd to resist. The crowd began to overpower the guard and started to reach to grab her.At that point, she gave a piercing crythen she woke up in abreaking cold sweat.Her personal guard, Captain uncle whose real name is Ashgard, was an endearing name which the Princess gave him since he was placed at her Guard by the King from the day, she was born she called him Captain Uncle, because he was considered as family to her, he was her favorite servant in the palace. He and Simbolelo the palace head securitythey rushed in the room swords in hand to assure her safety.

Ashgard and Simbolelo with swords in hands quickly checked the room as the personal maid Tiara rushed toward the Princess, who quickly reassured her that everything was fine, and she only had a bad dream. Once Tiara the princess's head maid heard the Princess account, she demanded that the men leave the princess room at once. They apologized and as they were leaving as ordered, the king and the queen rushed in through their secret passageto the princess' room with their guards.The king asked,"What is happening, my daughter? The princess replied, "Nothing,dad. I just had a nightmare."The king moved towards her and held her. He turned towards the guards and servants with a sign telling them to leave the room. Then, the king said to her, "My daughter, didn't I always tell you never to allow your subjects to see your weaknesses. You just can't allow that my daughter"The queen interrupted him and told her daughter that it is okay to be frightened from a nightmare. She hugged the princess and asked her to tell her the about the bad dream. The princess did and when she was done narrating, the queen said: "Darling, most dreams has its meaning. I hope you will be able to discover the meaning of this dream soon."

They made sure she went back to sleep then they left the room.

CHAPTER 2

Dreaming the Future

The following day, she went out riding horses.She rodeso fast that her guards couldn't even keep up to her.She performed many dangerous maneuvers such as jumping over obstacles and body of waters which some of the guards would noteven dare follow. While riding at such great speed,she barely missed a couple of paysan gathering woods.They dropped their woods and jumped out of the way in fear for their lives.She just laughed at them and continued. This left her guards were shaken up their heads in disbelief.

While she was having her fun, from a distance there were some suspiciously looking individuals watching her? She was riding very fast towards the palace. She noticed a tall hedge on the way.She made her horse hop over it.However, guards tried making their horses jumping over the hedge, too, their horses' legs were caught on top of the hedge some tumbled over, and some went flying in the mud. She halted her horse and took the time to laugh at them; the rode along only Captain Uncle was able to keep up with her.

She rode back home followed by the Captain through the forest, all the while under the prying eyes of the suspicious figures from the shadow.

A week after this event, she was having dinner with the king and the queen, she excused herself early from the dining table. Her worried parents asked why she was leaving so early. She simply told them that she was feeling tired and needed to rest.

She made her way to the bed laid by her maid for the night. Once again as she was sleeping, she began dreaming.It was the same dream from the last time. She saw herself being admired and applauded by all her subjects.Suddenly, their faces began to change from smiling adoringly at her to being mad at her, again a voice called from the crowd, "LET GRAB HER!"

However, this time, the guards did noteven try to restrain the crowd. Instead they also turn toward her and began to come after her too. She was frightened but she did not yell this time, she simply woke up without. She thought to herself,"I wonder what these dreams could mean. I need to find out what these dreams mean."

CHAPTER 3

An Unwelcomed Marriage Proposal

In the morning, shewent to talked to her mother, and explained the recurring dream.Again, her mother reminded her that most dreams have meanings. She suggested that she sees her dad's Prophet. They went calling the prophet to come meet with her for a consultation. Prophet arrived some time later that day, the princess explained the recurring dreams to him. After explaining, they asked for his opinion on the whole matter.The prophet paused for a few minutes to think, then he explained, "Well,the princess'those dreamsdo have meanings.Some part of it is easy to understand while the other part is difficult.He continued, your dreamsprincess has a single meaning."The queen and the princess got themselves ready to listen to his interpretation.

The prophet said, "With all due respect, princess, these dreams are your conscience reprimanding you for all the bad ways you have been treating your subjects,your people. I think you should do your best to change your ways, or else you could live to regret such action."

She laughed and questioned the audacity of the prophet."How dare you?Heinterrupted: No Princess, It's not me it's your conscience. Be quiet! the Princess ordered. How you know my conscience! How dare you tell me to change my ways?!" She added, "So you think a few bad dreams can influence enough to scare me into changing my ways. So, you think I am evil? You got to be joking?" He tried to explain, saying, "My princess, it's not me or what I said. Is what your conscious is revealing to you. The Princess said Enough "How do you even know what my conscience is like? Okay. I think that's enough. You can take your leave."

To the dismay of the queen as the Prophetleft, she began to make fun of him about the way he walks, talks, to insult the prophet.In the days following the consultation with the prophet, she didn't change but seeming gotten worse.

A month later, she was returning from her horse-riding adventure with her guards and her trainer and mentor, Captain Ashgard, she was all muddy from the horse ride. She noticed a beautifulroyal carriage with guards from the neighbor kingdom guarding it. As soon as she walked into her quarters, her head maid, Tiana, walked up to her and said,"My princess,a royal suitor has come to visit you. The queen, your mother, told us to come adore you and make you presentable so that you can come your royal suitor.

"What? Royal Suitor? I was not expecting any visitor!" She exclaimed. "And what do you mean my mother sent you to make me presentable, what does that mean? Does that mean I am not able to make myself presentable?" The head servant answered, "I am sorry, myprincess.That was not what I meantto say. I was just restating the queen mother's words." The princess took a deep breath and said,"You know something, you can all leave now. I' m grown enough to get myself presentable".Go and inform your queen mother that I will be right out to meet her visitor."

The servants tried to resist: But my princess, prince Terror and his representatives are here to ask you for your hand in marriage." What did you said prince Terror is here to ask my hand?" the princess asked in surprise."Yes, my princess,it's a royal visit that you have to honor with royal attires."The princess protested, "Hey, hey,enough already! I don't need you to remind me of my royal duties. Go tell the queen that I am coming." The servants again tried their best to convince her to allow them to help her get ready, but she wouldnot have it. She practically forces them out telling them she will get ready to come welcomes the prince.

Some minutes later, in the grand ballroom where king Jajah and queen Meme were entertaining the prince and his representative, the head servant came and stood near the side door, waiting for the queen to call her.The queen saw her.She signaled to thehead maid to meet her in the next room. The queen and the servant were talking at one corner of the room.The queen was not happy that the servant was not able to do was she ordered, she was telling her to go at once and make sure the princess look decent enough to meet the prince.As she was telling the servant that, the ballroom door opened. The royal announcer came in and announced, "Our beloved princess of Libertia…"Before the announcer could complete his statement, the door swung open. There was a huge collective gasp and looks of surprise on everyone's face in the room.Everybody faces was filled with an expression of absolute shock.

The princess came into the hall with her horse-riding clothes, which were all muddied. She looked very unclean; her hair was undone. The queen furiously yelled at her and yelled at her questioning her reason for appearing in front of her guests with such appearance. She said Princess Maelle what you think you are doing to come meet your guess in such condition.Maelle said,"My guest, I did not have any visit schedule with anyone until a few minutes ago when I heard that Prince terror was here? Then she turns and address Prince Terror. So,prince Terror, how charming are you to present yourself unannounced like this for this unscheduled royal visit."

The embarrassed prince said,"You are right, my princess.I thought since my father's kingdom, and your father's are practically neighbors, I would just drop by to come seeing you."The princess replied, "Oh, wow! You thought you would just drop by to come seeing me without any courtesy of royal announcement. Very charming!"

"Wow.Princess Maelle, I implore you to stop being so rude to our guests! I am very sorry, prince Terror," the queen exclaimed."Jah, are you going to say something here she asked."Finally,King Jahjah stood up from his throne and said:Prince Terror, I am very sorry for thisturn ofevent,there isobviously a break in communication here, because the princess was not aware of your visit here today. Please, excuse us as we must cut short this visit.We will now hold audience with our princess. We will be sure to extend you a formal invitation soon hopefully you will agree to grace our kingdom with your presence. Kindly relay my regards to your father.

Having said that, the king then gestured forhis guard to lead the Princeand his Representative out. Once the door closed behind them.The king turned to his daughter, and calmlysaid,"My daughter,you should know that your action here today is going to have grave repercussions, for our Kingdom".

The King said that because he knew how fragile the relationship is between the two kingdoms. It was never an equal relation. Libertia had been a very peaceful kingdom.Although they also have a great army, yet they never went to war with any other kingdoms. However, prince Terror's kingdom of Tretiawas an even more powerful kingdom whichhas had many conflicts with other surrounding kingdoms.Without any doubt, this unannounced visit to Libertia was a power move which was indeed meant as a sign of disrespect to the kingdom of Libertia.

The princess said to her father,"I am very sorry if I've embarrassed you and mother, but you raised me to be a person whospeaks her mind. You raised me to be strong and hold my head high no matter what." Then, she turned to her mother and said, "My dear mother, you out of all people should know how much I despise that man since we've been growing up together."

The queen replied, "I know you hate him from your childhood days, but both of you are no longer children, honey". She paused for a moment then said, "I remember when you were younger, the prince tried to steal a kiss from you, you decked him so hard and broke his nose". This small incident almost created a state conflict, because he was too ashamed that he got beat up by a girl, he told his people that he was attack by a mob in our country". "You can be sure that what you just did to him could be worse".

The princess objected to the prince's disrespect. She said,"But Dad, how dare he walked into your court without invitation like that father"? She continued, "But of course, you know dad that this act was meant as a sign of disrespect to you, your kingdom, and me right, Dad?" The king started, "Honey I know that, so that is why"!

"So that is why" she interrupted her father; "You should not tolerate his disrespect Dad". I never met a more repugnant man than this man, father". "How can he simply walk into your royal court like that and ask to see me, as if I was one of his paysan subjects? The King smiled with pride for her daughter as he continues to listen.

The queen interjected, "My daughter I know you despise that prince, but my daughter tradition dictates that you have to marry apowerful Prince to strengthen our Kingdom future. This is tradition!

"Really mother"? "Tradition, so you taught me to be my own person all my life meant nothing, in the face of this backward tradition, how can you tell me to conform to such a backward tradition, now? "Mom don't you think it's time we make our own tradition".

Speechless the queenregressed as she couldn't find a fitting answer to the princess question, "My daughter, all I can tell you is that your action here today is going to bring lots of grieve to our kingdom. "Jahjah talk some senses into your daughter, Excuse me." She left went to talk to Captain Uncleat the corner of the room while the princess turned to her dad. She said, "My dear father, please, tell me you understand?"

King Jahjah paused and said, "Honey, of course I understand, you made some great points. You are right.It was disrespectful of him to walk into my court uninvited as he did. "And no question they did that intentionally to show they have power over us. Honey between me you don't say this to your mother. I am glad you put him in his place, baby."

Out of curiosity, the princess asks if what her mother said has was the truth. The king admittedthat it might cause a lot of troubles for their kingdom, because prince Terror has been known to be a very proud man and will not allow this to slide like it never happened. "Therefore, without a doubt this incident will be the cause of great hostilities between our two kingdoms for sometimes to comebut as usual we will be managed.

 The king commended her daughter for standing her ground despite the consequences that may follow. He explained how glad he was by making them understand that they cannot be stepped upon as they wish.

The princess hugged both the king and the queen in appreciation. She left the room for her father and mother.

The king called upon General Simbolelo. He walked in and saluted the king as the custom demanded. The king explained the incident which just transpired between the princess and the prince Terror. Then, he orders that the kingdom's security be placed at the highest security alert. Simbolelo bowed as he said, "Your wish is my command, your lordship. Long live the king!" He went out and sent out the command to execute the king's order.

CHAPTER 4

The Kingdom of Libertia Becomes A Target

Princess Maelle was always known to speak out her mind. She was not an individual whohold her tongue except for her parents are concerned. Unfortunately, her straightforwardness got a lot of her subjectsand outside enemy mad at her. They did not hate her as a personally. Theyinstead did not like her ways of treating people. However, she was known for a single distinguishing factor.The whole kingdom wasaware of that factor. She was always willing to stand for the little guy.

The two kingdoms were under great tension after the princess rejected the prince of Tretia interest in her. The palace head guard, Simbolelo, gave orders to his soldiers to be on a high alert. Simbolelo reported that the rejection of the prince's proposal left the prince extremely mad at her. He wouldn't let it slip except he exhibits his superiority. The spies gathered genuine information that the neighboringkingdom was planning some sort of repercussion, but they did not know of what kind.

After issuing out an order to his officers, General Simbolelo called Captain Uncle and spoke roughly to him. He said,"Captain, I need you to take your job seriously and get a handle on the princess because her latest action has put us in great hostilities with the Tretian Kingdom". Get her under control or resign if you can't." The Captain was not happy with the way Simbolelo addressed him.He said to the general,Get her in control General How? Am I supposed totell her how to behave?" "You are responsible for the safety of the king and Queen?But the king put me in charge of the princess, to protect her life, not to control her, with all due respect General I will do what I was charged to do, protect her life, nothing more.

Simbolelo said,"Captain, let's make one thing clear to you the royal family safety is my responsibility,it means every member of the royal family not just the king and the queen.

I know you are favored by the King. But until I am relieved of my duties and you are placed in my position. I oversee this whole kingdom; every standing officer will obey my command. And that include you. Did I made myself clear to you, soldier?!""Yes,sir!" the Captain answered. He continued, "I did not mean any disrespect,General. I was simply trying to make you understand that my relationship with the princessdid not authorize me to get involve in her personal affair." The General interrupted,"Enough of your relationship with the princess.We all know you have a close rapport with the Princess.Just follow my orders, Captain.Okay, Captain?""Yes, sir!" "Dismissed soldier." The Captain walked away.

*****

One faithful day,the princess was moving down the street with her cortege. People were going through their daily activities.Some were selling fruits, some were selling vegetables, and others were buying.The streets were bustling with business as the royal cortege was making their way through, her Avant guard horsemen was announcing and yelling at the people to get out the way to allow a free passage for the princess.

At that moment, a middle-aged woman who was selling bags of fruits in her hands was about to cross the street when someone cried out,"Watch out!"Voosh!the horse brushed against the lady even though the Avant guard did his best to avoid hitting the lady sending all her fruits flying into the air then she fell to the ground. The head guard ordered that the princess carriage be brought to a stop. He commanded that the soldiers secure the princess then bring him the person who put the princess life in danger.

The princess curiously, peeked out of the chariot and asked the Captainwhat happenings was out there.The Captain explained that a lady defied the order from the Avant guard to clear the road.He mentioned that due to her disobedience, she almost caused harm to the princess. The princess yelled at him in disbelief, "You mean she defied a royal order?!Where is she?"

When people saw the princess coming out of her chariot,they started whispering to each other how the woman was done for.Someone said, "Oh my God it's the Princess, that lady is finished… So,she went over to the ladywhen the lady saw her, she dropped to the princess feet crying and lamenting, asking for forgiveness.The princess yelled, "Stop, just stop your begging." She reminded her, "Show some courage because you are a citizen of Libertia, every citizen of Libertia must be courageous". She ordered the guards to bringher along with them.

While they were leading her to the carriage, there was a commotion within the public gathering.Some people were trying to restraina younger lady from advancing toward the scene, others were encouraging her notto say anything because she also risk being taken away by the princess too.This young lady was of big stature.She simply pushed everyone holding onto her away and ran toward the guards while demanding that they release her mother.The guards noticed the big lady advancing towards them, drew their swords in a defensive formation to protect the princess.While the older woman nowpinned to the ground on her knees shouted, "Jane!Do not come closer.Stay back! I will be fine."She said to the princess, "Please, princess, I will go with you. Please do not hurt my daughter. She may look big in stature, but she is only fourteen."

The princess said, then told her to order her daughter to put her hands up and not resist my soldiers. The princess said,"She is also coming with us." The woman made an effort pleading to the princess, but she wouldn't listen. The Princess said it's an order, I said she is also coming with us. With little or no option left, the woman said to the lady, "My daughter, do not resist the princess' guards. You are coming with me. Don't worry we will be fine."The guards grabbed her.They put the young lady and her mother in the carriage with the princess. Two of the guards tried to get inside the carriage to protect the Princess against the prisoners, but the princess objected stating she will be fine.

The Captaincame to the princess, explained how dangerous it could be to leave them in the carriage without guards. He tried to explain how dangerous it would be to leave them with princess, but princess became a little irate at the Captain and said,"Captain, are you refusing my order? Are you defying me? Are you saying that I can't handle myself against these two?"

The Captain replied, "Of course No, myprincess. I know more than anybody that you can handle yourself, but since you are not armed, I thought it would be a difficult task to guard them on your own."Maelle gave him an intense look. He quickly readjusted,saying, "I am sorry, princess, Iam too overprotective of you sometimes." Maelle said to him with a warm face, "I understand,ok Captain to put your mind to ease.Then just give me a machete."They gave her one then she said, ok are we good now? He simply smiled then she said we are ok then "Let's get going… she said, they mounted their horses, she got in the carriage with the prisoners and they left. As they left."As they were leaving, the people together with her guards began to say amongst themselves how more dangerous she is than her father.

*****

CHAPTER 5

The Conspiration Against the Princess

The following day at the neighborhood kingdom of Treatia, Prince Terror who was still fuming mad because of Princess Maelle's rejection. Prince Terror was walking back and forth talking to some of his advisors, he said in a loud voice: "Whodoes she think she is to refuse my proposal like this?That is an insult to me and our kingdom. I guarantee you this will not stay without repercussions." I need you to think about how we can strike at them… as they were talking

There was a knock at the door, the door open. The announcer proclaimed the arrival of a group of subjects from Libertia to see the Prince. Prince Terrorsaid,"Oh!Let them in."They led them in.The prince welcomed them and said"Welcome,welcome my friends, welcome to Freedom, my kingdom is now your kingdom. You made the best decision of your lives to renounce your Libertia citizenship and adopting your new Kingdom of Tretian. They walked toward the Prince and bow down at his feet.

*****

Back at the kingdom of Libertia, the princess was again out with her guards.This time, she went undercover, dressed like a regular soldier. The soldiers did not even know that she was a girl or that she was the princess.Except for her private guard, Captain Uncle, who knew who she was.CaptainUncle oversawthe troop,and the undercover soldier princesswas placed second-in-command of that troop.

While patrolling the town square, she noticed that a strange event was about to occur.There were two unlikely criminals and two young ladies, the oldest about 17 years old, and the younger about 14 years of age. She watched them discussing a little before they went their separate ways. While patrolling, the princess didn't take her eyes off the older one. She watchedher closely as she walked weaving in and out from stores to stores. Finally, she noticed her looking toward her young friend with their fixed, the older one signaled,and they both turned around and fixated their ways toward a rich-looking man with two big bodyguards walking down the street.

The undercover princess watch as the older girl began to make her move.She went toward the man, acting as if she was begging for money.The princess focused on what was about to happen.The rich man began to laugh at the girl along with his bodyguards. He grabbed her hand and pulled her toward him.He proceeded to tell the girl something in her ear. The girl got offended so she slapped him.The man stepped back a little, and motion forward to grab the girl.

Shequickly gave him a big chap in the throat called a rosette.As the man was falling to his knee on the floor coughing and wheezing trying to catch a breath, she quickly grabbed his money purse from his side. When the guards saw that, the first guard launched at her.She extraordinarily flattened him with a leg flip.The second one quickly grabbed her from behind. She quickly slipped down by doing a split on the floor.She grabbed his hand and flipped him over her head.This extraordinary feat shocked everybody nearby.

It certainly got the attention of the princess and her guards.They yelled at the girl to stop,when she saw them, she quickly ran away from the scene. The Captain ordered three of the soldiers to go in pursuit with him after the runaway girl.He orderedthe remaining soldiers and the princess to remain there, but the Princess who was their second-in-command watch the runaway girl as she was running and weaving in and out through the crowd. The princess kept watching and following her through the crowd. The princess noticed that as she ran away, she was going toward that younger friend from earlier,they lightly bumped against each other, and continue running.

The princess noticed the younger friend simply got up from the ground, dust off her cloth,look at the money purse which was switched to her then walked the opposite direction.The princess understood that the money purse had been transferred to her. She ordered thesoldiers who were with her to come with her quickly.They followed the younger girl from far, as she was calmly walk away, weaving betweenhouse to house out of the city.She led them to a well-guarded compound within the forest. She entered the house after being waved in by two watchmen. The princess, together with the soldiers, followed her to the house situated at the center of the forest.

They spied over the compound for a while and noticedthat people around the compound were leaving their houses to get into that center house. The princess and the four other soldiers infiltrated the compound. They started by putting the gate watchman to sleep with a chokehold.She signaled two of the soldiers to go to the back of the house to secure and prevent anybody from escaping. Then, she signaled the other two to follow her into the house.They stealthily neutralized the outside guards in front of the house.They busted into the house, ordered everybody not to move. She mentioned that the compoundwas surrounded by the royal army.

Upon hearing that, three older ladies and two younger girls who were in the house stood up and unsheathed their machetes, preparing to fight.A voice from the bedroom within the house call and said,"STAND DOWN and OBEY THE LAW". Then an amputee came out limpingfrom the room.when the soldier took a closer look, they realized that they were standing in the presence of a greatness. This was the house of a past most valiant warrior General whom all the soldiers recognized and apparently really respected, so with excitement mixed with disbelief, they said, "Is that really you my General, is this really you, they all went over to him to greet himand shake his hand except for the princess.She did not know the general so she tried to call them to order. She yelled,"Soldiers!Stand your ground!"One of the soldiers objected and tryexplain the situation to their commander. "Commander, this is General Pemba. everyone thought he was dead. He is a great general. Which everyone respects and admires. All of us soldiers want to become a great warrior like him."One of the soldiers turned to the general saying, "General, how it is possible that you are alive and no one knew? For the past years, everybody thought you were dead." The General answered, "As you can see, I am still alive.""My general, you must come back to take your rightful place.""No, the time has not come yet my brothers.In factI am going to ask of you a favor.Please, don't tell anybody that you saw me here."

The General noticed that he did not recognize the commander standing with them. Thus, he inquired,"Commander, I don't think we've met before."But before the princess could talk, one of the soldiers jumped in and said,"My general, he is our new commander. He is a young new promoted officer. That is why he does not seem to know you."

Amid the dialogue, one of the soldiers who was posted outside walked in with the Captain.The Captain did not even notice the General.He went straight to the princess,saying, "Your soldier told me that you tracked that girl accomplice to this house. I'm so proud of you, my trainee. I trained you well.""The other girl led us close to this compound and simply disappeared into the forest right before our eyes."The princess answered, "Yes sir" The Captain continued "I am glad you followed her accomplice here she will eventually have to show her face here, I am glad you followed your training well."

As the Captain was congratulating the princess dressed in military attire, he heard a recognizable voice who said"If you've trained him well, who trained you?" The Captain turned around,questioning the voice that came from behind. The voice replied,"Who else but your old trainer." He looked around and saw General Pemba. He was shocked, and his mouth dropped as he saw General Pemba he said, General Pembais that really you? My General?" He went over and said,"Yeah,it is you,Oh, my general, I'm so glad to see you alive?" He saluted him with much reverence. "Sir, everybody thought you died. What happened to you?" General Pemba said,"Captain, I know you very well, and I know most of your soldiers here. I know I can trust most of them. But I don't know about all of them here.Before I can tell you anything else, I must ask you, can you vouch for all your men here?" The Captain answered in affirmation,saying that their loyalty cannot be questioned. He said, "We all owe our lived to one another. Yes, I trust all of them here with my life"

The General said well then we can talk, However, before the general start talking the captain interrupted him and said, "General before we say anything else, let me begin by telling you how sorry I am about your family. Sir, after I heard that you were dead, I did my best to support your wife and girls financially, I continued to do so for months, until one day I went to your house and found out they were all gone. I'm so sorry I failed to protect your family.The General answered, "I appreciate all you did for my family. The General, "Don't be sorry because my family is all fineCaptain,because I was the one who sent for them". The Captain said,"Really?Oh, I am so happy to hear that they are doing fine." The General continues, "You see Captain, I felt their lives werealso in danger, and because you were the one supporting them, you were also putting your life in danger" because the same people who wanted me dead were and are still out here. So, I had to make them disappear, just like I had to disappear.They are all here.Here is my wife, the first girl and Rod are still out there, these are my younger girls, Tiarra and Jaffa, Oh wow that is little Tiarra, and Jaffa I did not even recognize them.The General said, " YesI trained them to fight and to survive."

The Captain was surprised at how fast the daughters have grown. He explained how he wouldn't have recognized them if he found them outside. The Captain explained how the older one showed her robust skills in beating up two bad guys and disappeared from the site. With pride written on the General's face, he affirmed that the lady mentioned is his daughter. Then,the Captain asked, "Then, where is Rod, you first and only son? The General answered that Rod is on a special mission for him.

The General continued, "You see Captain, I believe that my kidnapping was a well-orchestrated act." The Captain was surprised and said in disbelief, "What General so you were kidnapped? Yes, my friend I was set up to die but somehow my life was preserved. It's my belief that our Kingdom, and possibly all our other Kingdoms in this continent may be in great Danger. "Yes, my friend, I was set up to die, but somehow my life was preserved. But what is worse I believe that our kingdom, and possibly all our other kingdoms in this continent may be in great danger. You see,an outside enemy may have infiltrated our kingdoms in Africa to the highest level. They have been working very hard to cause a rift amongst our kingdoms while presenting us with the hand of friendship. While stabbing us in the back because they knew if they can divide us, then we will not be able to stand together against them. Their plan is to divide us to conquer us."

The captain said, outside enemy what do you mean by outside enemy General? The general answered I 'am talking about non-African people infiltrating our continent. The Captain said are you saying that you were kidnapped by these new strangers?

The General continued, "No,I can't say for sure who kidnapped me. I just think that we don't know enough about these new people to give that much access to our kingdoms." The Captain replied,"I understand your concern general, but so far, they have been very friendly.So, why do they have to be apprehensive ofthem,General?" The General said,"What I am saying is that we just don't know enough about them to trust them that much." "Well general, from what I understood, the white men have been coming to do a fair exchange for our spices, our silvers, and our golds. And in return, they provide us many useful tools which we need." The General exclaimed,"You said Fair exchange,how can we be sure their exchangesare really fair?"What if what you called a fair exchange was not fair at all?

Captain, I trained you to think past any situation, right?" The Captain looked puzzled but answered,"Yes,my general!"

The General continued, "You asked me why am I so suspicious of these new people, it's because of something that happened when I got kidnap. Then one of the kidnappers told me something that I have never heard in all my life on this earth. Since thenI began to think, "What if thesenew people were coming here for something more important than gold?" The Captain looked confused and seemed lost. He thought for a while and said, "More important than gold, but general what could be more important than gold and silver?"That was exactly my thought my friend when that kidnapper told me that, the general continue "That is the question that I have been asking myself to, but I amsure we will find out sooner than later. What the General did not tell the Captain was that he sent his only son andother spies to investigate the white men present in this area."

The Captain said, "General, the ways you talk give the impression that you think they were the one who kidnapped you, if yes why would they do that? "Listen, Captain. I never said such thing, I have no idea who was kidnapped me, but I like I said I will find out sooner or later their biggest mistake was letting me escape". "Yeah General so, how did you manage to get away"?The General answered, "To tell you the truth, as for how I got away, my memory is still a little vague on what I am about to tell you right now but listen well maybe you can help me make sense of this whole event. "When these peoplewhom I could not make out their origin kidnapped me, something strange happened. They took me to a house deep in the forest, they had a translator who spoke our language, and I tried to bargain with them. I explain that I am one of the richest men in the kingdom, I told them that I was willing to give them their weight in gold and silver if they would let me go. But when they heard this, they laughed at me. They said that what they were here for was something more precious than gold and silver." Can you believe this these people refused golds and silver?

The captain said, "I must say that this is really incredible! But go ahead and tell me how you got away?

"So,when I heard that thenit became clear to me that these people were absolutely not interested in my gold and silver, Iknew I had to get away if I wanted to leave, so tried to get away someone hit me in the head from behind, when I came back to myself I woke up dazed and confused inside this strange beast apparently at the bottom of the sea, because I could hear the wave crashing against its body. I thought either I was dead or that I was swallowed by a big fish because of the fishy smell from the inside that place. I later realized that I was at the bottom of a boat. I somehow managed to get my hands half free. Then, I made my way to the top of that boat towhere I could breathe some fresh air. Once I was outside catching some fresh breath,I realized that the boat was full of many other people apparently tied up. I could hear them yelling and crying from a compartment under the boat. As I was about to go down to help them, I heard this big boom noise. Then, I was hit with what I believed was an arrow with a fire on his tip. I fell in the water and start swimming toward the shore. I heard many other boom noises. Unfortunately, one of those arrows on fire hit my leg. I was losing so much blood that I lost consciousness. Days later I woke up daze and confused, itwas the people who saved me from drowning who explained that the damage to my leg was so severe that they had to amputate my leg to save my life. I tell you it still feels like I am in a terrible nightmare."

The Captain said, "Generalagrees that this is a nightmarish story but,although I don't it will make much difference, I willpresentyour concern to my superior general Simbolelo. But,I fearthat hewill not want to believe me because he so dislikes me."

General Pemba said, "Oh yeah that's true. I head Simbolelo is my replacement.I'm glad he finally got to be the general as he always wanted to be. Even though I believe you were better suited and prepared to be my replacement than that guy. I never trusted him anyway.My advice to you will be that you shouldn't trust him that far."

"That's true, general Pemba.Everybody was so surprised how quickly he moved through the rank to get to your position.Sometimes, I wonder if he was not involved in whatever happened to you." General Pemba said,"Who knows?Everything is possible, but as I am still living sooner or later, the truth will come out."

The General continued explaining, "You see Captain, this is the problem we have too many people all over this continent who are toopower-hungry are willing to do anything for power. Some are now promoting opening our borders to the strange people in the name of free trade.

After the General finished to narrated his experience, the princess, having forgotten that she was an undercover soldier, spoke out and said,"Captain, all that story was great, but we have a job,to do and it is getting late.We must take the prisoner according to rules.We must take them in for questioning." The general abruptly stood up and turned toward the soldier,he said,"Soldier, how dare you give an order to your Captain? Captain is this how you train your subordinates these days."

TheCaptain realized that theGeneral was right, not wanting the princess to blow her cover, he said to her, "Soldier, come over there with me." He led her to an unoccupied corner of the house.The Captain told her very apologetically with the lowest tone of voice, "Excuse me,princess, for talking to you like this,but you will need to apologize to the general and me because you do not want to break your cover." She said to him, "Are you crazy?""My princess, your work as a soldier is too important to stop now right? She thought for a minute and said,"Okay,you right I want to maintain my undercover work, but we must take at least the girl with usbecause you know our army's motto is *We always get our pursuit,*"if we don't bring in a prisoner, it would be a sign of lost for us, and you know what could be the consequences.

The Captain said,"You are right. So, they walked back toward the General and she said I am sorry General, and Captain. So the Captain added General the soldier was right as you know our motto, *"We always get our pursuit"*.So, please allow us bring your daughter in for questioning.I guarantee you that. I will get her back to you safely."

The General did not objectbecause he the army rule, but he requested that the Captain should promise that he will not allow his daughter to fall into the hands of that mean and evil princess because the news of her ruthless reputation has been going around the whole kingdom. He said, "I heard that she's even tougher than her father, the king of Libertia. The Captain simply smiled while looking at the undercover princess.Then, he said,"Yes, that's what I heard too".In any case I guarantee that your daughter will come back to you safely to you."The General nodded in affirmation and went to have a little chat with his little girl. The General said,"Don't worry ok, my young soldier.I want to assure you the Captain here will keep you safe and bring you safely back to me soon." She said to her father,"I know, father. I'm not worried about going with them." That's my soldier!

The troops left with the younger daughter. The older sister was watching them from the bushes where she hid. When they passed her, sheready herself to attack from behind and fight them to free her sister, but someone grabbed her from behind.She was held and subdued, with the other hand covering her mouth.She wasn't able to make any noise. She struggled to free herself, but her attempts failed.After the soldiers were all gone, the person let her go. She quickly pulls her knife, readied herself to fight her aggressor.Then, she recognized the person which she thought was her aggressor was none other thanher own brother Rod.

She screamedin disbelief, "Oh my goodness brother is that really you, Oh, my goodness Rod I can't believe you are here.

Yes little Sis that is me, How is Dad, how is everybody else? Rod answered,

Dad is good brother but that was our little sister that you just prevented me from rescuing from these soldier. Sister you could not fight all these soldiers even with my help. We will get her back I promise. What did Dad always teach us? She answered almost sarcastically, yeahyeah" Live to fight another day. Exactly the brother responded.

Come on don't worry about our little Sis, she is only 13 years old, she will be fine what do you think they are going to do to a 13-year-old girl. Torture her or something? Come on sis…

The sister said, "You never know, from what I heard, on how that princess has become so evil. Seriously sis It's Maelle that we are talking about, we were raised with her she was never as evil as people make, it seem.

The sister answered, "Like I said you never know because people do change." Rod laugh and said, "Whatever girl let's go back home I'm sure Dad will tell us how to proceed. So, she hugged him again. Then they started walking home… He said by the way Sis you know that you are losing your touch right, I can't believe I was able to catch you off guard like that" "Like I said brother, I was just too focus on attacking those soldiers I did not noticed you coming". Anyways, he said let's go home. (They continued home)

CHAPTER 6

A Princess Like No Other

In a cell, deep under the palace,the sound of girls yelling grunting and crying was heard echoing deep inside the castle dungeon, like people being tortured, with lashes and ringing of machetes...Those noises were loud enough to get the attention ofall the servants around Castle. Sometimes later,there was a bang at the prison door.The posted guard opened the prison door, and the princess walked out sweating with her hand bloodied. As she made her way down the aisle of the castle, she noticed the servants and even the soldiers were hiding moving away from her. Others made a way to avoid crossing her path as they were terrified of her.

Meanwhile, at the kingdom of Treatia palace, prince Terror, who was still mad aboutprincess Maelle's to him,was still boiling when they announced him that his spies were back from the neighborhood kingdom of Libertia. The prince entered the room; the spy bowed down to his feet and said, "Myprince live forever." The prince replied,"You can stand upmy most trusted friends. I am so glad you are back here safely."

The spy went ahead to report the information gathered. He said, "First my prince, we have good news.I, together with the other spies, spent two weeks in their kingdom, gathering in disseminating bad information about the princess.I must say she is still loved by some, but lately, she is beginning to have many enemies then friends.Her people are starting to see her becoming more and more ruthless.They mention that she has been arresting and taking people from the street mostly young girls and they are never seen again. Some say there are more than thirty-five young women who have been taken by the princess."

The prince replied in surprise, "Really but how come the parents ofthese missing children have stayed quiet about all that"? The spy said,"Well Prince the fact is most of these taken children are either from the streets or orphans"therefore they have no family member to complain about them missing. The Prince replied in amazement, "Wow she is an evil genius that girl! That makes me love her even more". He exclaimed, "Great work mypeople, indeed this is good news that her peopleare beginning to turn against them. Now the time has come for our final attack to destroy them so I can take her for my slave queen."

The spy replied, "My prince, you know you can always count on my honest advice and expertise. I owe you my life and my career, but sir, I must be frank with you. As we all know, their army is as strong and well trained as ours, so excuse me for asking this."How we will be able to attack and destroy them, and my prince, you know your father will never go for that plan."

The prince replied, "My friend, don't worry about that. Leave it all to me. As we speak right now we have someone at the highest level inside the Royal Castle working for us. You know, my father is very sick right now.It's just a matter of time until I ascend to the throne, as for the rest of the plan on how we will be able to attack and destroy them; the perfect plan is already in the working". "However I will let you be a part of the firstpart of the plan. Here it is." He said while presenting the plan to the spy. "I will need you to continue to disseminatethe lies about the princess, telling people that she taking and killing young girl and using their blood to take bath blood so she can remain young and beautiful forever.

The head spies ginned, and greet the Prince then walked out, assuring the prince that the work will be done to his satisfaction. Then, the prince mentioned that he would communicate the rest of the plan with him in later time.

That night, the prince left with cavalry to a secret meeting.They changed their clothes, rode all night until they reach an area by the sea where the prince andtwelve of his body guards boarded a ship.They were led by some strange-looking men.

Few of his guards watched with amazement these strange looking people that they were meeting for the first time of their lives, some of those guards never met any of these strangerscalled the white men. They were perplexedseeing the white man's skin color. Some they were very puzzled.

Then, the prince called them to order, "Men,regain your composures.They are men just like you and I". They simply have lighter skins just like the albinos." The Captain of the boat laughed vigorously and said afterward,"Men,like your prince, said, rest assuredthat we are men although we are nothing like you people. He said all smiling"The boat Captain then greeted the prince with respect and welcome him onboard. "It's a pleasure to receive you on our humble ship my Lordship." With his broken English language, the prince said,"Yes, I am happy to see you too, my friend. The boat captain said, "Wow, my prince! Your English has greatly improved sincelast six months that we have been doing business.""Yes,

I have been practicing with the Indians and other Arab teachers which you have provided us with. Now they are also teaching many others people in our kingdoms

The Captain said,"Okay, let's get down to business."The prince ordered the guards to leave, and the Captain ordered the crew out.The Captain proceeded to say, "Now prince, the plan is ready.What about your side. How is the king?" The prince answered, "You know my father is a fighter; he is really sick but still fighting." The Captain mentioned,"Okay, take this and give him some.Then tell me about the outcome later." The prince took the little bottle, put it in his pocket. Then he said,"I have all your favorite drinks here with me. I will have my crew bring the cases to your waiting chariots."

The prince handed him the plan and mentioned he would start sending merchandise to him starting in a month. The boat captain nodded in agreement and greeted the prince as his future king.

Chapter 7

Something more important than gold?

Back in the Ex General Pemba's compound in the center house people gathered around to listen to Rod adventure, the ex-general seem puzzle he said, "Son I really don't understand this. What do you make of this whole thing? Dad like I said I have never seen anything like this Dad, the brutality was so extreme the sad part was that some of these people doing this were our own people. Dad it was horrible sight to see they had our people in chain young and old.

How did you happen to discover this son?

Rod explained, "Ok Dad you remember the jamboree that all the surrounding kingdomsalways have every years, so my friends Terrio from Tretia, you remember him?

General Pemba said "Oh yeah Terrio, the one who look exactly like Prince Terror. Yeah I remember him, "So what about him?

Rod said anyways Dad, so as I was saying you rememberhow busy that party usually is, General Pemba say "Yes." Well not this year Rod continue, we began to hear talk about many people becoming missing here and there from our different kingdom. So as we began to inquire more so we found a surprising fact although all the surrounding areas were having many people missing However Terrio found out and verify that only theone kingdom thathas not had anyone missing. 'Which kingdom is that" the general asked? It's our neighborhood Kingdom of Tretia.

So the General said," Well did you find out why the Kingdom of Tretia is the only Kingdom who has not had missing people.

He said.' No dad, however we left many spies in the Kingdom to investigate.

The general then said, "Wow isn't that something, because since a few month ago people in this Kingdom have been reporting people missing. Which some people thought was the Princess doing. But now that you tell me this is happening in all those other Kingdoms and territories now I know that is definitely not the Princess.

Dad come on please tell me you was not about to also believe the nonsense people have been saying about the Princess.

General answered, Listen son after what happen to me I must admit that I don't have much faith in anyone anymore especially not in these Royals. In factI know my captain has giving me his word but I am becoming very anxious about my young daughter's faith with that princess.

Dad come on, we personally know the Princess in fact I was practically raised with Princess Maelle from the time you were her father's head Personal guard. She was practically born in your hand you know she could never be the monster they are saying that she is. At least I will never believe it until I have my own proof.

General Pemba said. I used to think the same son but no anymore, since after the way I was cast aside, by King Jahjah, son people change sometimes. Look how close I used to be with her father the king. In fact I would be shocked if he was not personally involvedin my demise.

Don't think like that Dad, Now why would the King be a part of that? What could he have gained by destroying the person who saves his life so many times?

I don't know! Rod my son you are just coming of age, time will teach you more about not whole heartily trusting people.

Anyways Dad I am going to the King and Princess tomorrow and tried to shed some lights into all these crazy talk about the Princess. Son I know once you made up your mind no one can change it so all I am going to tell you is to proceed with care. However one thing before you tell anyone about your finding find Capt Uncut and explain everything you told me, make sure he give you back my girl to bring back. As they were talking, their look out come to announce that there is apparently a soldier from the palace riding toward their compound, so Rod come out to meet him. When he saw that was Captain Uncle. He welcomed him in the general came from his room to meet him.

Good afternoon General, the Captain said. ?"First, let me assure you that your daughter is fine, and as I promised, I would bring her back to you as soon as possible.

Okay Captain, by the way, you remember my Son Rod,

Captain said Oh wow Roderick, man you are turning into a big man, General these young people are making us look very old.

The general said, "So true, so true my friend, so, tell me to what do we owe this visit from you?" "Oh yes, my general, I am bringing you some shocking news about the Royals! The Captain exclaim.

What, what going with the royals? The general asked.

We received news that King Chad from the Kingdom of Tretia has die, and our Kingdom Royals has been invitedto the Coronation of Prince Terroras the new Kingtwo days from today.

"Prince Terror as King, "This is indeed shocking news". The general agreed. "CaptainIt looks like things just got very complicated", general Pemba said while looking his son.

Rod interject, "Captain, don't tell me that the whole royal family is thinking about attending that Coronation.

"They do not exactly have a choice here, sir. The Captain explained. Not participating will further escalate tensions which are already on edge since the Princess just rejected Prince terror's courtship and marriage proposal.

Shocked by the Captain's statement Rod said, "Hold on, did you say Princess Maelle just rejected the prince's marriage proposal? Turning to his dad, he asked, Dad why am I just hearing about this? Observing that general Pemba remain silent to that question, he said to the Captain, "So, you mean to tell me that Prince Terror came to propose marriage to Princess Maelle, and she turned him down.

Yes, son, she turned him down. Since then, the relationship between the two kingdoms has been on edge.Rod said Ououiiii. I love that! I am impressed by the Princess's decision Rod declared happily So captain, I hope after this whole deal with Prince Terror I hope that the Princess is not actually going to that Coronation right?'.

TheCaptain said,"I am really not at liberty to say much. Still, the truth is Ireally don't know because you know how strong minded she is, should she decide to go no one could stop her.

Rodsaid, "Oh No she should be convinced not to go, that Prince is so vindictive who know what he could do, yeah. Rodcontinues. What about that mirror image of her that she uses from time to time that is why some people think she is magical. They believe that she can be in two places at the same time.

The Captain said,"I believe that is the plan, but as I told you, she is the only one that make that decision. The funny thing is, and your father knows this very well too, if she does decide to use that double none of us will be able to guess which one is traveling with us".

"Yeah, these two look so much alike even I was never able to tell the difference, only her mother and Dad could differentiate them." General Pemba commented,

Yep okay, then gentlemen, I have to go get our people ready for the trip. One more thing, do not make any move until I come back, please. I guarantee once I am back, I will have all the power and capacity to personally make sure that your title is restored to you. You will regain everything you and your family have lost. You have my word. He said as he mounted his horse and galloped away.

As soon as Captain left, Rod turned to his Dad I know that Captain said no to make any move until he comes back Dad I know sure we trust him and everything, but I'm not going to sit here and wait, while we let our fate get decided by others.

I am going to the Princess early tomorrow,hopefully, I will be able to convince her not to travel for the Coronation. If things difficult, I will make sure I freed and bring my little sister back home. Rod said with determination.

General Pemba worried about his son'sstubbornness he said, "Rod I know once you have made up your mind, no one can change it, but please you must proceed with care, and if you do encounter the Princess, first make sure you are dealing with the real one, before you tell her anything.

Dad, "I know how I can differentiate them". Rod said with confidence. "You do? how can you differentiate them? General Pemba asked. I have my way! He answered while smiling.

The next day, Rod group met with Terrio group, he thanked Terrio for coming with him for the mission, however the time it took to wait for Terrio's group cause them to be late in going to the Capital, while in the route to the capital, they observed from far the Royal Caravan who was already on its way to the Coronation, Although Rod wanted to stop them to talk to the Princess his friend convinced him that would mean suicide because the Royal guard are Stealthily trained to defend the Royals against all odd, He watched in anguish as the King and his Army pass along. Thus he decided if he was not going to prevent the princess from going he was not about to leave his little sister lock up somewhere in some dungeon. They quietly made their entrance into the Kingdom Castle thru a hidden passage which the princess showed him when they were younger. Once inside they were extremely surprise how the kingdom was left absolutely unguarded.

Again Rod thank Terrio his friend for coming with him but he told him that seeing how much unsecured the Palace was he would not need to stay with them. Rod said, "I am happy to have you with us, Terrio. But I'm astonishedhow easy it was to access the Royal Palace. 'It's crazy that the King's palace only had just a few guards. We did not even need to bring all these people with us. So I think I can take it from here, you can leave if you want to. "Rod you know I owe you my life, so I am happy to support you till the mission is accomplish". Terrio cut Rod off to say.Rod said, "That is so true I saved your life", Rodlaugh and say Thanks brother I appreciate your help here. Although you won't get to play the part for which I brought you here let at least go free my little sister. Go left I will go right, let me attack first, wait then come in only when I call you inside the dungeon where they keeping the prisoners.Rodand Terrio each went their ways.

As Rod was getting closer to the dungeon, he could hear a young girl wailing, and yelling from inside the Dungeon.

He had a gut feeling that it could be his little sister being tortured. He said, "Oh man, I swear that had better not be my sister that they are torturing like that. He quickly overpowered the guards which were guarding the front door. They busted inside that court place brandishing their machetes. Shockingly, he found his little sister was on the back of the Princess as she was straining herself, yelling as she was doing a push up with her on her back meanwhile the noises he was hearing was from the other girls who were training hard fighting against each other with wooden machetes.

When they heard the intruders, they all stopped their training. The Princess quickly rolled over from under the little girl, and thengrabs her machete. Sheorderedthe girls to get into formation to protect themselves. In a majestic choreograph gymnastics moves, all the girls fell in a spear-like fashion with the Princess in front of them. They were pointing their machetes toward the intruding group. Who are you? And how did you get in here?" The princess yelled at the intruders.

"Guards! She screamed, but none came. Rod judging the impressive situation quickly stepped forward and said. "I am sorry, Princess, for barging in like this. I thought my sister was being tortured". "Your sister, who is your sister here"?The Princess asked. At that same moment, Tiara finally recognized her brother. Rod, is that you? She asked, not waiting for his reply, she rushed from behind the Princess to go to him. The Princess tried to stop her, but she freed herself and ran to Rod. "I have missed you so much brother," she said while hugging him. Wow, Rod? Is that you? The princess asked, moving closer. She said, "Oh wow that is you Rod, I almost could not recognized you with this bear. How are you? How have you been? I am so happy to see you".

Rod said, "Princess I wish I could say the same about you, but I'm not even sure that'sreally youwho is in front of me.The princess answered,"What, what are you talking about Rod? Of course, it's me, Princess Maelle. If you are the Princess Maelle, so then tell me something, who was that Princess Maelle that I saw leaving for the coronation ceremony this morning? Rod, you out of all people should know that this is a state secret. I cannot answer this question.

Princess, It's me, Rod, your childhood friend. Don't you trust me anymore? Rod, of course, I trust you. The princess responded. "But being my childhood friend, you of all people should know whether you are looking at the real Princess or the fake one. Princess Maelle, we don't have the time to play this guessing game. If the real Princess is on that trip, she may be in grave danger. "I understand, Rod, the princess answered, but I am Sorry. I wish I can tell you more, but unfortunately, I really can't". Telling you could put our Kingdom in Jeopardy.Rodso, you really won't tell me, right? Rod said,"Okay, then you leaves me no other choice. Only one person can help reveal this secret.Rod turned around and motioned forTerrio to come out. My friend, you can come out now. At that moment, Terrio walked in.

When the Princess saw Terrio walked out she was shock and discussed. Thinking he was Terror, the princethat she so despise. Her face changed from normal to being extremely mad. She quickly picked up her machete; she ordered the girl to stand guard and menacingly pointed it toward the Prince.

She yelled. "How in world did you get in here Terror? What the hell are you doing here, I swear you won't leave with me here alive. Girls,be on your Guards, get ready to fight for your lives. She commanded the girls with her. Again, in many majestic choreograph gymnastics moves, all the girls fell all around the Princess in a spear-like fashion with the Princess in front of them all of them pointing their machetes toward the intruder. I don't care how you got in here, but you will never take me out of here alive! I would rather die here than to marry you, and as for you Rod I am so disappointed of you. The same sort awaits you.

Immediately she made that statement, andRod stepped in. There it is this is the truth that I was looking for. Thank God; it's you, Princess Maelle. Thanks, Terrio, for your help. Rod said.

Very puzzled, the Princess said, "Wait, what? What truth? Why did you call him Terrio? What is going on, Rod? "Princess, I am so sorry, I know you have many questions. However, this was the only way I can be sure that you were the real Princess". Rod said apologetically

"What are you talking about Rod, I don't understand? The princess shouted.

Princess, I am sorry for putting you through all this? I had to use my friend, Terrio here to help get the truth from you."Rod explained to the still bewildered princess. This man is not PrinceTerror. He is my best friend, also from Tretia; he is the lost half-brother of Prince

Terror. Iknew that you would never tell me if you are the real princess so knowing how much you despise Prince Terror, I had to use him to find out the truth."

"Oh, my Goodness, are you serious, Rod? But he looks exactly like him".

"Yes, because he is prince terror's half-brother". Rod answered. He was raised by a poor widow after the Queen of Tretia killed his mother who was also her sister. The story was that his mother was the queen's twin sister. One day the King took advantage of her, she became pregnant. She kept the secret for eight months until the day the queen found out. The queen instead of helping her had her removed from the palace and ordered her and the baby killed. The assassins stabbed her in the stomach, missing the baby by inches, and left her for dead. A poor widow found her and helped the mother give birth before she died. So she raised him but never tell him the truth up until she was about to die.

Long story short, here he is today looking very much like his half-brother but the complete opposite of that monster Prince Terror. Anyway, I am glad it was not you on that trip because Prince Terror is planning some mischievous things for your Kingdom. You see,we got confirmation last night that that guy is up to something , so that was precisely why I came here to tell you, unfortunately I saw the Royal cortege leaving I was afraid that it was you and not the double on the way to that coronation. So we came here to confirm which one of you was in that carriage."

The Princess said, "We argued about it all yesterday, I really wanted to go to protect my Dad since for continuity reason my mom was to stay behind, but my mother knew they could not stop me from going. Last night she tricked me and purposely gave me a sleeping tea. I just woke up Three hours ago to find out that they left almost 12 hours ago by now they should already be getting in the capital, so I am stuck wondering and worrying to death about my father". The princess worried said.

Rod, do not worry, Princess. We have our spies all over their Kingdoms. They will be sure to come to the aid of the King if need be and also let us know if things get out of control.

That's good to know. Anyway, I' m still mad at you for tricking me like that, the princess complained while she playfully hit Rod.

"I am so sorry, Princess, but you left me no choice". She playfully said. "You know me I will get you back Rod" "I know I am scared already Rod answered,

I know you will try;I have to keep my guard up. Hahaha, they both laughed, and she ordered the girls to get back to training. Rod said, "Wow I am really impress with what you have done with these girl, they are scary good, and all this time people have been going around talking bad about you, saying so many mean things about"

The princess said, "I know they said I eat people heart, the new one I heard was that I take blood bath to say young and beautiful.

Rod, "Oh my goodness princess you heard all the hurtful lies and you did not do anything to stop the lies." What could I do, show them how I took most of these girl from nothing to make them into discipline fighting group. No they can continue to tarnish my image but one day these girls will guarantee the security of our Kingdom."

"Princess I am glad you said that because there is another important matter, Rod.On our way here, today I noticed the Capital and the Palace security is very lax.

Yeah this morning I found out thatUnderstandably the General took many of your elite guard with himto protect my father, but we heard that there was another order given to many of the remaining soldiers given them permission to go home for few days, leaving the capital and the palace very vulnerable. Of course I have ordered them back, but it's going to take a while for them to get my message and get back.Rod said, "Okay then if you don't mind Princess, we have many valiant men with us here I can have them guard the Kingdom, especially here in the palace tonight, until all your soldiers are back just as a measure of security. He concludes. The Princess said, "Sure, you're welcome to stay until then". Princess Maelle said excitedly.

Chapter 8

The great betrayal

At the Kingdom of Treatia Palace, Prince Terror was rehearsing his coronation ceremony, when they announced that his insider from the neighbor Kingdom of Libertia is here.

The Prince entered the room, and the Spy bowed down to his feet. My King, may you live forever. I have a message from my commander for you. Okay, so how is my general? And my most trusted friend. The soldier answered, "he is well my King" Sir, my commander wants you to know that the Royal family is en route and will soon arrive for your Coronation.

Well, I assume that's including my future queen, right?

Yes, about that, my King, my commander, wants you to know that there were discussions whether to have the real Princess, or her double representing her in the Coronation. However, he believed as you know that the princess is strong-minded, he believes that she most likely overruled them. The spy answered.

What do you mean by her double? Prince terror asked, curiously.

Well, sir, what I' m revealing to you now is of utmost secret.The likeness or double is a security trick that our army came up with where the King the queen and the Princess have people who look exactly like them, trained to be to replace them during a specified event that deems too dangerous for the Royals. Prince Terror said. "Wow, this is a great trick; this is one that I will add to our Security tactic".

So, soldier,is your commander 100percent sure that this is indeed the princess, my future queen and not her likeness who will soon be here? Prince terror asked.

Sir, my commander, believes the princess is strong-willed and would do what she wants. So he believe there is a greater possibility that she is the one who is coming her However, he can't be 100 percent sure but told me to tell you that he knows how to verify if that is really her or not. He said he will reveal the secret to you personally when they get here.

"Ok, so tell me when are they arriving? The Prince asked".

"They should be here in a day, the soldier answered. "Ok follow my adviser". They will take care of you. The prince dismissed the guard and motioned for the advisor to let in the other guests. A groupof white-armed men entered.

Long live the king, my King, thank you for your reception, Mr.Blanc, the commandersaid.

You are welcome. Here is the map of Libertia. As we agreed, do not burn or destroy anything; just take the people you want and leave the Kingdom. Do you have everything ready? Because as we speak, they are on their way here. When will they get here exactly? Mr. Blanc asked.

"They would be here in oneday." The prince answered. Great, so my king, as we agreed, I congratulate you in advance because, by tomorrow you will be the King of two kingdoms.

Let our agreement be known to all your friends out there that after this transaction. We don't want to see any of your people in this region unless they get my permission, understood? Prince terror said arrogantly. Understood.

"We completely understand, my king".

Ok, you may take your leave now. The prince dismissed them. Then the prince Generals, I need you to pass this order down, after this week, if any of you ever see any of these white people in our region, be ready to fight for your lives. The General said, Yes, my king lives forever. One more thing generals once I become king tomorrow. I want all of you to publish the following announcement that the Kingdom will be doing a competition to find the person who looks like me the most; the winner will be given lots of wealth.

They all answered Yes, my king, we will publish it two days from now. Then they left.

*****

Chapter 9

The betrayal continues

The country of Tretia was in a great festive mood. The day of the Coronation was the following day. The Royal family of Libertia wasen route with almost all the army at hand while they were travelling to Tretia. Unnoticeably on the other side of the river, there was a contingent of white traders with some black Tertian soldiers going in the direction of Libertia.

General Simbolelo kept riding next to the Princess Carriage and looking inside the Princess carriage, looking for anything different about the Princess. The Captain who was sitting in the carriage with the Princess asked,"Do you notice how the General has been checking up on you during the trip?""Yeah, but why though"? The princess answered. Well, the General is trying to make sure that it is you the real Princess and not your double that is travelling with us". The captain said. But the Princess simply laughed and said, "That's lovely she admitted. "So, people really cannot differentiate us. I am so enjoying this" She asked, So what about you, Captain? Don't tell me you can't differentiate us either." Princess Maelle, the captain started, I must admit it's challenging for even me who knows you since you were a baby. Even can't distinguish if this you or your likeness? So I ask," Please tell me is this really you"

"You just called me Princess Maelle. Therefore, you must surely know that I am the real Princess Maelle. So then why are you still asking me, Captain?

"You know you can trust me, princess. Telling me will help me to better protect you. The captain pressed further.

"Oh, now, I see. So the real reason why you want to know if I am the Princess is so that you can discriminate in the way you protect me. Either way, I can't tell you because it could put someone's life at risk.

The captain replied"You know that is not true, Princess. I just want to know so…..

"Enough Captain, I am done talking about this, is that understood? The princess interrupted him

"Yes, my princess. The captain answered

Later that evening they finally arrived at the palace. The prince was looking at them from his upper room window. General ordered his soldier to be on their best guard. The Captain also told the Princess's security to be on high alert. A few hours later, the Prince called his advisor. Listen, I want you to send word to my Guest. Tell General I need to see him tonight. Yes, my King. May you liveforever.

Later that night, someone was walking down the hallway. Inside the Prince's office, an advisor announced, my king, live forever. Your special friend is here to see you. The door opened, and the person walked in and bowed down,"Welcome my most trusted friend. I am glad you made it safely. What news do you bring me?

At that point, the spy who had bowed down with his face still down said my king live forever. I have so much information for you. But before everything I have a complaint. Well, stand up and speak your truth, my friend. The spy slowly got up to reveal that he was none other than Captain. Ashgard, So, he continued. My king, guess who I just found out is still alive the other day?

Out of curiosity the princeasked, "Who".

General Pemba! replied the Captain shockingly he is still alive and in hiding. Your people failed at kidnapping and eliminating him as you promise me.Worse of it all is his position was not also given to me as we planned; the Royal gave the position to General Simbolelo.He complained bitterly

 Are you serious? General Pemba is still alive? This is indeed veryunexpected and disappointing news. However, since he is still not in power and is in hiding, he poses no threat to you or to our plan. As for you not being chosen General in his place, it was a miscalculation on our part. Anyway, Simbolelo, it's no problem. Once I become King of our two United Kingdom's the position will be yours. In fact it will be even better because You will be the Governor of the Libertia Kingdom.

"You right My King thank you, my King, Captain, replied and continued, so concerning the plan, when I left the kingdom, I made sure to remove all the Palace guards, which makes the kingdom very vulnerable for the easy take over! The captain said.

"Great job Governor! The prince said, so, you are sure that they will not have any resistance even with that little band of bandit that the Princess have been training?

The captain said,"Sure they are good, but I am very sure that without her being there to lead them, they will be easily taken down."

Prince replied , "Good to know, so when you said she would not be there to lead them, does that mean that you are 100 percent sure it's her and not her likeness that is here with us? "Because I tried to take a careful look at the princess when they came, and I still couldn't tell the difference, but I was told that you know a secret way to tell apart. So, what is the secret? The prince asked.

The captain said only her father can tell you if she is the Princess. So, we may have to result to torture him to get him to talk, but I guarantee you he will talk one way or another. Ok my prince   I must go back before they suspect anything. Liveforever, My king.

As he was leaving the meeting with the Prince, a spy of the General was following him. Later that evening, the spy went to talk to the General about the Captain's secret meeting with the prince.

The next day, the day of the Coronation. It was the most dazzling festive atmosphere. The ceremony went fine, and the time for the reception came. There was a special wine given to only the guest. The General strictly ordered all the soldiers not to drink, but early that day the Captain made sure special bottle went to them to drink. He told them it was best to get a little to drink now since they wouldn't be able to drink later. In the reception, the general made sure he did not drink anything and gave formal orders for none of his Royal guard soldiers to drink. Unfortunately, he was not aware that his Royal guard soldiers had been coercedby the earlier captain into drinking. Unfortunately by the time he knew it, they were all already compromised.

Chapter 10

A Sad day in Human History

The Reception was almost at its end the LiberianKing and his Army had retired to their quarter the guards started fallinglike flies. They were not aware that their drinks had been laced with sleeping drugs by the captain. Throughout the night the Tertian soldierswere just picking up the libertian soldiers who fell asleep, capturing them, removing most of their uniforms, chained them then transport them to the awaiting to the slaveharvesters'boats.

After eliminating the whole Elite guard in the outside barrack, In the middle of the night, Captain entered the Libertia Royal quarter with some Tretian Soldiers dressed in Libertia elite guard'suniforms. Seeing that it was the Captain, the guards on duty let them in,so the captain and the men surprise attacked them, however one of the royal guards escaped to go tell General Simbolelo and sounded the alarm he told the General that they were under attack by the traitor Captain. The Captain soon arrived, and his men, the fought and killed the first line of defense. General Simbolelo, with just two dozen of brave guards, broke through the traitor's line of attack with the King and princess, killing a greater amount of the enemy as they were in the court about to leave with the King and the princess; they realized that their Chariot was damaged beyond repair. Captain Ashgard intercepted them and engaged the General and his men into a terrible machetes battle.

General Simbolelo, was very angry at his Captain betrayal, cursed him out. "You coward and you traitor! I will bury your body here and take your head back home for them to see what we do with traitors. In the middle of the fight, the captain tricked the General by acting like he lost the fight and was asking for pity. When the General went over to finish him off, he quickly produces a long knife and kill the General, but at that same time the General also injured him mortally. They were taking the King to King Terror Castle when Captain Asguad started crying, "I am cold, I don't fell well, I am dying, please don't let me die, don't let me die, I want to be the Governor, I want to be the Governor. Then he stopped breathing. The Princess watched him with disgusts as he died, she simply said, "Good riddance you Coward!The put them and shackles to wait for King Terror

Sometime later King Terror arrives to see King Jahjah in shackles, he scorned at him.

King Jahjah realizing that it was indeed King terror who ordered the attack, demanded answers he said, "Prince Terror, what is the meaning of this?" The King shouted

"Its King Terror nowthanks you very much". King Terror answered arrogantly.

"I demand you release us at once and…". ""King Jahjah started.

Quiet! King terror interrupted. "You demand? Listen, I am the only one here who can demand or command here". So, I have some demands for you, King Jahjah. If you answer correctly, you and your daughter will be spared. you understand? King Jahjah nodded, "Yes"in response. I know the Princess, your daughter uses a lookalike from time to time, yes don't be surprise I know a lot more than you know.So I demand you tell me the thruth, I will ask you this once King terror said, pointing his machete at the Princess, "Is this lady here, your daughter, Princess Maelle, or the fake one? The King was about to answer when King terror interrupted him. Be very careful not to lie to me because lying to me will cost lives here today, as I said. Is she your daughter?

"Yes she is my daughter, Princess Maelle." "You are sure? King Terror asked again."I swear on my life. She is my daughter", the king repeated. Okay, since you swore on your life, Okay I believe you. Then King terrorsaid;"Now for my second demand, he pulled a piece of paper and handed it to King Jahjah, he said "I need you to sign here to waive and pass your right to your Kingdom of Libertia to me."

 King Jahjah looked at him with repugnenace and asked, "You are joking right" Do I look like I am Joking"? King Terror said with a straight face. "You must be out of your mind! King Jahjah concluded. "You are Crazy, look at yourself, you need help" King Terror calmly nodded his head in agreement and say, "You know something? You are probably right. I must be out of my mind, to think we could do this transfer of power peacefully". At that same moment, King Terror went slash with his machete and severed the King ofLibertia's throat, his body dropped to the floor. The Princess in anger, yelled, "King Jahjah!! Why did you have to kill him? The princess yelled. You are worse than the monster that people says you are!" You are a cold blooded killer". King terror stood, astonished by what he was witnessing, he noticed that she called her Father King Jahjah. And not,Father, second he noticed while she was mad and yelling and cursing at him she was not crying for her dead father.

"Wait, just one minute, something is not right here. I just killed your father,you yelled and curse at me but you didn't even shed a single tear?

No no, I know they say that you Princess Maelle is heartless but even you can't be that heartless, for sure you must be the fake princess. Something is not right with this. Guard get her and keep her tied up and take her to my chamber, I will make you talk one way or another,

Meanwhile, in Libertia, everything was calm. The whole kingdom was asleep, but Rod was still up reviewing and making sure that all the Post were well guarded, and so was the Princess. , they met.. During the process, Rod and the princes met at the garden palace, and they timidly approached each other. Rod, who was surprised to see the princess awake, asked: "Why are you still up; I told you to go to sleep."

"I am a big girl now I can take care of myself". The princess answered

Rod said, "Oh come on my Princess, you know I did not mean it that way. I remember very well how great your skills are. You don't have to remind me that you used to beat me up when we were younger. But I am much better than I was ten years ago. He added, smiling.

The princess simply said "Rod, I'm grateful that you are here to help, even after what happened to your dad. She continued, especially because my dad did not do more to help your familymuch when you needed it the most. The princess added.

Rod answered "I am here for you, princess despite your father or my father, "Rod for me? The Princess asked, surprised at Rod's confession. "Yes, for you! Rodreplied. Aww, that is so sweet of you! I appreciate it. She stepped closer to him and reached to kiss him on the cheek, but he turned and stole a kiss from her. When she looked surprised, he started awkwardly. "Oh, I am sorry, Princess I shouldn't…. She placed her finger over his mouth, "Shut up and kiss me," the princess urged.

They began kissing tenderly for a whileuntil a guard interrupted them, "I am sorry,Princess.We have intruders in the Kingdoms" Get everybody up quietly and be ready to fight them. On the North side of the Capital Rod's people took as prisoners another group of white and Tretian soldiers. On the South side Tretio's People first took as prisoner the first group. All the palace guards, Rod men, and the girls readied themselves to fight. As they saw a group of soldiers HoweverRodask her sisters Tiara and Challa to stay behind, but the Princess told Rod to give them a chance and watch. He agreed and watched with attention as the girls walk out laughing and giggling and laughing, so the intruders thought they were party girls. The intruders waved them over when they got close enough toengage the men they approached the girls, making kissing gestures at them. As some of them reach to touch the girls, the girls in just a few minute flattenedthe all of them to the floor with some acrobatic fighting maneuvers.

When another group of soldiers,saw what happen,they point their gun, so the girls turned and retreated back to the unguarded palace leaving the gate and door open. The soldiers blindly followed them in; once they entered, they found themselves surrounded. The princess ordered them to all dropped their weapons and kneel, which they did. Rodand Terrio grabbed one of the Tretian officers and asked him what their plan was here. The officer refused to speak, saying he would rather die before he talks. Rod told them to put the rest of them in jail.

They blindfolded that Tretian Officer and put him in a separate cell. In the middle of the night, he heard some people fighting and speaking his language. They told him that they were here to rescue him. After seemingly fighting their way out, they finally got out of outside the capital, inside the forest. Someone took out his blindfold and said well-done Officer when he opened his eyes. He saw that he was surrounded by Tretian soldiers. You did well for not revealing our secret. Come with me inside. Someone wants to reward your bravery. He replied, who is it? At that moment, King Terror appeared right in front of him. The Officer dropped to one knee, head bowed down, "My King, Live forever.'

"Well done, captain, king terror said. I am sure you guys did not know I was going to come supervise the mission. I am just trying to understand why the mission failed. So, you understood what you had to do here, right, if yes give me resume of what your mission was to see if maybe, we missed something? Yes, sir Iunderstood. the mission clearly,"You asked us to capture all the able body men, give them the sleeping drinks bound them, and transport them to the Coastwise and the lightning vessel in the port to be exchanged with the white people for their precious metals. You also ordered us to take the metals back to you in our capital.

So, if you people did understand the mission, why did you guys fail so bad? Explain to me the mission.The officer answered" Well, sir, Captain Ashgard guaranteed us that we would not get any resistance,that was totally false. We will need more soldiers than what we came with if we going to take over the Libetian Kingdom as plan. So since you are here my king, does that mean your plan to get rid of the king and Marry the Princess worked?

When the Princess who was behind the door heard him said that, she got extremely mad she was about to go over in the next room to kill that officer, but Rodmanaged to hold her back. He hugged her then she started sobbing, father, Father. "I swear if Terror hurt my father, he will not live to regret it."

That officer who was not aware that he wasbeing tricked, continued to expose all the secret not knowing the person that he thought was his King was only Terrio, the king's lookalike.

Terrio asked "Where is the remaining sleeping drink to gave to the prisoners? "In the Chariot, my King" he responded. Terrio then ordered him bound and sent to be exchanged with the white men.

Rod ordered the guard and all the other Tretian soldiers be taken away,undressed and be given the drink and the same treatment which they reserved for them.

Rodtold his men, "Dress up like Tretian soldiers. Take theTretian prisoners and put them in chains. He said, "We are going to give them the same end they planned for us. Rod men then took them to the white men on the boat and made the exchanges and brought the metals to Rod.

Chapter 11

A Historic payback

The Princess and the queen were crying uncontrollably. The Princess was fuming mad. Rod and the girls tried their best to console them. General Pemba, now back in charge put the Army on the highestalerts.

Now that it was clear that King Terror was the major reason why all these people where disappearing from all over, General Pemba send report to all the surrounding Kingdoms, that people were being kidnapped by the white strangers with the help of King Terror and other warlords to be sold into slavery in their country. General Pemba declared,"Our fight from now on is to stop this evil trade and make all the culprit pay for their crime.

The Princess vowed, "I swear Prince Terror and all his accomplices will pay for their crimes against humanity." My poor dad! I wonder how much he suffered.

Princess, "Princess your father's fate yet, Rodtry to comfort her,"Please try to rest and regain your strength, tomorrow we take action".

Rob walk out the room leaving the Princess resting, he went over to talk to his father. Dad this criminal must pay with his life, you should convince the Queen to declare war on them. General Pemba said, Son I know you are furious right now and you want to make this guy pay, but if we go to war, we will cause too many unneeded casualty and destructions, the slave maker would just continue their evil trade with a different King, beside we got almost half of our army in their hand, no son we must be smarter and come up with a better plan to put a stop to all this craziness. General Pemba reason with his furious son. "Go get some rest sontomorrow we will meet with the Princess and come up with a perfect plan".

King Terror called all his General to prepare to invade Libertia, however his General told that all the surrounding Kingdom heard that he probably the one who killed King Jahjah, His Chief General said, "They vowed to stand with Libertia to fight against you if you attack them, You most high King we advise you to play it smart and go the route of Diplomacy. So, he was advised to send his emissaries to explainto Libertia that he was not the one who killed King Jahjah. Theemissaries reported to Libertia with the rest of the King and the body of all his dead Guards which they said were attack on their way home by Rebels. When General Pemba inquired about the missing soldiers, the emissaries announced that they were captured.

Later that evening, after planning the Princess came out with a most genius plan.

Terrio dressed as King Terror with his men dress in Tretain soldiers uniform broughtthe capturedTretian soldiers for tradewith the white men. When the white men saw them arriving, the captain went to welcome them. "Oh, my King! He said" To what do we owe this unannounced visit, My King? I thought you said once you become King you will no longer come make these trades.

"I needed to see to it first end, that these Royals of Libertia are gone" King Terror answered. I have about 50 prisoners here ready for the exchange. Soon I will send you many more.

"It's an honor to do business with you, my king" The captain said, excited.

"Tell me in which boat did you put the people of Libertia, I am about to send their Royals to you too, and I don't want them to be put in the same boat with their subjects." King Terror inquired.

The white captain answered, "My King they are all on the boat North of here

So, Terror ask, when will that boatleave the port?

The boat captain answered" It's full and ready they will leave first thing in the morning,sir.

"Good. I am sending in the final batch tomorrow morning," King terror

Did you say final, my King? The captain asked

Yes, since I am the King now, I have made new rules. Tomorrow will be our last trade, after you leave tomorrow, do not return. I have been gathering your riffle,and Ihavesigned treaty with all the neighborhood Kingdoms. We have decided to end this sort of trade transaction.

"Oh no, my King, are you sure? If it's more profits you want we are willing to give you more profits. The boat captain pleaded.

No, it's not a question of profit; we no longer want to do this sort of business after this last trade, tomorrow, we are done. Is that understood? When the guards noticed how angry the king was, they pulled out their machetes to pressure, the captain, sensing the gravity of the King threat, he quickly agreed to the King's demand, he said, "Yes, my King, I promise this would be our last trip here!

The King left the room, but Rod stayed behind to talk to the Captain he said, "Listen Captain I know our King is very moody today, but trust me,first he is not mad at you, second he is certainly not serious about ending this very profitable business. "He is currently having woman problems, and you know that the woman he loves, the princess of Libertia,don't want anything to do with him. That is the real reason why he is so mad.

Listen this is what you should do to fix that situation and retain his friendship and business. Send a formal invite to the king at his palace telling him you are having a great and lavish western dinner for him and all his trade partners from past and present trade deals, telling him that this big party in his honor and Elevating him higher than any other in this continent. You know how he loves western gifts, also, tell him that he will be presented with the mostlavish western gifts!

The captain said, "Wow I'm loving that idea already!

Rod said, "That is not all here is the part that will not be able to resist, tell him that your people have managed to kidnap the Libertian Princess, which you will also offer to him as your special gift to him. But ask them to keep this party in the utmost secrecy, to not attract attention to you guys' business dealings. I guarantee you that this will change his mind. Rod added.

The captain was happy for the advice and promised to do as Rodsuggested, but he had one objection he said, "Listen I love all your advices, butone problem we have, no way to get to the Princess of Libertia; how can I promise him that? Rod said, "Don't worry, about that, I guarantee you will have the Princess, I will personally bring her to you here,do your part and I will do mine. They both agree so the Captain promise Rod, if this work that he will make him rich, Rod nodded then left.

Later that day, the king was meeting with his generals and officers when his special royal messenger arrived. They led him to the King Office he said,Oh my king, live forever. The messenger said. "My King I have a special invitation for you, sir, of the utmost importance.

When he heard that he ordered everybody, "Leave us, we will continue this meeting later. He then turns to the Messenger, "Ok my trusted messenger, what is the special invitation about.

The messenger said, "My King live forever, the invitation is from the whiter traders, they are giving a Lavish western dinner to honor you in front of all your other trading Partners and investors. They also added that they have many great western gifts, the likes that we have never seen.

"Tell them I appreciate this, but I am not in the festive mood now, I don't think I am going" King terror declined.

But my king, the messenger interjected, "they wanted me to tell you that theyhave the greatest gift, that you wish to have the most in this world." The greatest gift that I want the most in this world" The King questioned? Yes, my King, the messenger said while smiling, "Theyhave the Princess of Libertia, bound and gag waiting for you.

What? How? That is impossible, they have the princess. The King exclaimed with great interest as he stood up. "Yes, my King, I saw her with my two eyes, bound and gag, fighting and fussing inside their boat.

"Are you sure it was her that you saw, because you know she is known to use double? Yes, my King, the boat captain, personally showed her to me, as she yelled and demanded her release, they got her with the help of your spies, I spoke to them they are Tretian. My King, you know I have been your Royal messenger since I was a young man, you know you can always trust my message". The messenger said. Okay, but you understand as King now I can't take any chances. Therefore, once this whole thing about the Princess has been verified. I promise to reward you and honor their invitation.

Immediately after the messenger left, the King Head spy entered the room.

"My kinglives forever, I have some news. "What is it? Speak at once! The King responded.

We just received word that the Princess of Libertia has disappeared. Apparently, she was so saddened about her father's disappearance. Against the advice of her head security detail, sherode her horse in the forest without any security.Now, the Royal guards and her security detail are going all over the country looking for her. How do we know she is not one of those fake ones? No, Sir, she is not the fake one if she was, they would not put that much resources into finding her, there is no question that she is the real one.

The King thanked him and told him to keep him informed of any change in the situation. He picked up the invitation again and read it. The king called his Royal messenger again and gave him a list of all his biggest business partners to invite to the exclusive reception given in their honors. There were about 30people.

KingTerror insisted that they only come with their close bodyguards. These were all trading partners involved in this inhuman trade. They were mostly military Generals, officers, many warlords, other rich people. It's only for them and their close guards, make sure to remind them and also add that they treat as top secret. King terror insisted. Yes, my

King, live forever, the messenger said, and left. The King smiled and told his guard, as usual, get the regular six soldiers to accompany us tonight.

Chapter 12

Restoration of Humanity

At precisely 8 PM, a large contingent left the palace in the direction to the port, where the party was to be held. When they arrived at the boat, the head security posted soldiers around the ship so that the secure the area, before the King can exit the chariot, a few of them went on the to check things, then the give the all clear the comes down, he is welcome by the Boat captain, the boat was beautifully decorated,. When the King entered the ball room, he saw all his friends were already waiting, they all stood up and applauded him.

Meanwhile, outside in the dark, the noise of a quiet attack was barely notice by the guard posted on the boat for more security "vouch,vouch, vouch, vouch,vouch,,vouch" these were the noises six arrows, which quickly eliminate the king's first security details on the North side of the boat, another six arrow quickly eliminate another six security details on the Southsideleaving the King a sitting duck in the boat. The Boat captain stood up and welcomed and gave a toast to the king, "You are very welcome. We have prepared all of this in your honor, my king." The captain said, pointing towards all the beautiful arrangements in the boat.

They all got up and lifted their drink and make nice wishes to the King. Everybody, including the King the bodyguards, drank, not realizing those drinks were lace with sleeping drug. After they dined and drank more wine, the boat captain gave the king a special gift,a gold-plated pair of guns, all the other guests applauded. The King thanked him.Then the captain said my King as I promised your best, most cherished gift is inside the room tithed up and waiting for your Honor.

When the King heard that he, got up to go to the back room at once accompanied by four of his body guards leading the way, when they got in front of the room the boat Captain motioned for the king to enter, but the four guards following him rushed in front to check the room and verify that it is safe for the King to enter. They saw the Princess tied up on the bed. When the princess saw them, she wiggled and shook herself angrily trying to free herself. Once the king sat eyes on her he grinned and again he thanked the boat Captain, He immediately ordered all his guards and the captain to leave them at once.

King terror arrogantly walked over to the bed where the princess was tied and whispered, "I had the fake one. It's going to be such a pleasure to have the real one now.". A few minutes later, the king heard some loud thumps outside the door. He rushed over and opened the door to find a mirror image of him standing and staring straight at him. The King was absolutely dumbfounded. While he was trying to gather his senses, he heard a girl voice from behind him, saying, "YOUR EVIL REIGN IS OVER. he turned around rapidly, he saw the Princess standing up unbound, Before he could react to try to grab her, BOOM Tretia hit him over the head, he fell like a piece of log.

Meanwhile, on the other boat which was holding the Libertian people, on the North side of the port, the white boat captain noticed some of King Terror soldiers bringing what looked like more slaves for trades, all tied up to each other. The surprised captain got down from the boat to go question the soldiers and tell them that his boat was already full, but the soldiers told him those teenage girls are gifts from the King for his crew's pleasure, to show his appreciation. The Boat captain happily yelled out for his men, "Looks like we are going to have a lot of fun on these trip boys."

All the crew members from the boat started shouting and whistling at the tight up girls. They started to select the girls according to their preferences. As the men led the girls up on the ship, Challa, who was the girl's leader, started smiling as the soldiers left them with the white slave master, knowing what she was about to do to them.

Back at the party, Terrio, now dress in King Terror' attire, came back to the party, he thanked all the guests saying, "Thank you all for your nice gifts, but he turn to the Captain said, "As I already told you, Captain and I maintained it, this is our very last visit here. Once you leave here tomorrow.

When he said that all his partners along with the Boat captain were very shocked at the King statement. They began to grumble. The king ordered everyone to be quiet, as he continued to say, "By the way Captain, I give you all these people here around this table and their body guards for free to take with you. As soon as he said that, there was a commotion around the table as they started to try to get up to get their weapons, Rod's men rushed the room with weapon in hands pointed them at the people around the table and the white crew members.

The Generals, the officers, Warlords and their body guards, the all began to feel drowsy they began to said "What is happening to me" Why am' I, feeling so drowsy," Some of them start crying, my head, some cried my stomach, and I don't feel good. When they tried to stand up they start falling. The King told them, "You people don't worry yourselves about fighting it guys; you all have been drugged up. After they all fell down, he ordered the white crew member and his other men to undress them and chained them. After that he said. "Now you white people I give you but a few hours to get all your trashes and leave my country and never come back.

A few minutes later, a guard came to report to the Boat captain. That the boat on the Northside caught fire all lives and properties aboard are lost.

So he told his guards "Make sure you bring them that extra special gift too ok! So some of his guys stay behind to make sure this boat leaves our port in 3 hours' The King said you got three hours or your boat will also perish here, then the king left....

Moment later it was daytime the waves were crashing against the fast moving body of the boat which was now in the middle of the ocean, by that time Boat captain was waking up on top, as well at the bottom of the boat the sleeping Generals, the officers the Warlords and their body guards were also waking up from their drug induced sleep. When they realized where they were they began to yell, scream, cried and fight trying to lose the chains which were biding them to one another, so they begin to yell curse you King Terror. All the noise finally managed to wake the most important person on that boat, King Terror woke up saying. What is going on? What is this place? Why Am I in chains? No, no, no, this must be a nightmare! He yelled Someone yelled. "Curse you Terror, You put us here". He shouted "What who the hell said that to me? At that point the person next to him looked and said guys, you won't believe this but King Terror is next to him said, "Yeah it's all your fault, you did this to us. He said King Terror why did you do this to us. Another one yelled, "King don't call him King, As soon I get a chance I will kill you myself Terror". Another yelled No I will kill him first. Look at you now you sold us now they got you here too, that's good for you. You are dead man Terror… I swear I will kill you myself Terror The King realizing his predicament started to bargain with his angry enemy, he said., " Don't worry my friends it's all just a great misunderstanding I will call the captain and to get this thing straighten out. Captain, Captain, Someone said "You are waiting your breath this people don't come down here. So he starts yelling, Captain. Captain, get me out of here, you made a big mistake, I am the King, I order you! Captain, get me out of this hell. I am not supposed to be here. Captainnnnnnn, Captainnnnnnnn...His voice echoed in the vast ocean.

A few days later, King Terrio, together with Queen Meme, and Princess Maelle gave a solemn proclamation to all Tretian and Libertian citizens.

I'm here today with Queen Meme and Princess Maelle to proclaim a total and absolute ban of all forms of slave trade in our two Kingdoms. I will work to persuade all other kingdoms to also do the same. Also, I will take this opportunity to ask you, my people, for your forgiveness. If perhaps due to my ignorance got coerce into letting this type trading with the white man happen in my kingdom. I have created an exceptional military service which will work to identify anyone who was or is still engages in this illegal trade with the white man.

As you have noticed, many of our great general and officers and others great fiends are missing today. It is because these unscrupulous white traders have taken them. Today I ask for your help; to report anyone who is involved in evil trade. I myself was almost a victim of that trade too but for General Rod who help rescue me. Thank you, General Rod. The king commanded. "So, I urge everyone to work together to stop this in human practice in our kingdom". As a sign of my good will today, I'm releasing all the prisoners of wars taken as slaves.

I also command that all our big food storage be opened so that a fair measure of food is given to all the needy citizens in our kingdom in exchange for them to perform community services. If they are incapacitated by old age or health issues, a fair measure will be given to them for free.

Finally, I want to officially offer my condolences and also apologies to the royal family of Libertia here present, Queen Meme and Princess Maelle for the terrible loss of their king. Everybody commended the King's speech, and all went home singing his praises.

Later that day, the King invites the princess the queen and Rob where he thanks, and speaks his heart to them. He said,"My Queen, my friend Rob here has something on his heart that he would like to reveal to you and the Princess, General Rod you have the floor." Rob said, My Queen, I thank you for giving me the blessing to do what I am going to do now.

Princess Maelle looked at her Mother with confusion as General Rob kneel down in front of her with a beautiful ring and say, My beautiful Princess Maelle with your mother's blessing would you do me the great honor and become my Princess, lover and wife forever.

She looked at her mother happily smiling, the Queen nodded, she then turn to General Rod and say," It would be my honor to be your Princess, your lover and wife, with that said Rob got up put the ring in her finger, King Terrio and Queen Meme joined the hands to that of Princess Maelle and General Rod to show their approval of their union.

The End

Praise God Always

www.ingramcontent.com/pod-product-compliance
Lightning Source LLC
Chambersburg PA
CBHW081230020426
42331CB00012B/3108